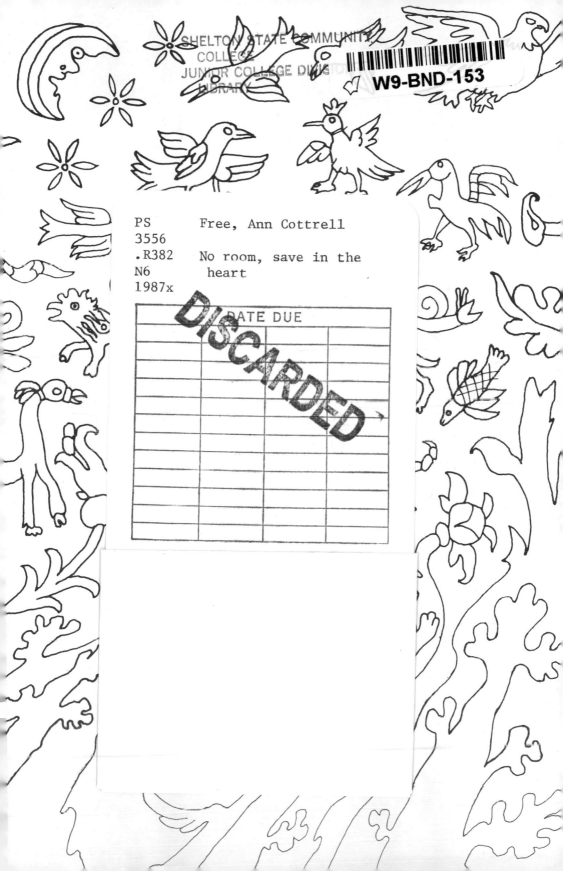

NO ROOM, SAVE IN THE HEART

I

NO ROOM

SAVE

IN THE HEART

Poetry and Prose
On Reverence for Life—
Animals, Nature & Humankind

Ann Cottrell Free

The Flying Fox Press

III

Note from Publisher, The Flying Fox Press: The flying fox (Pteropas poliocephalus) is a vegetarian fruit bat commonly found in the Southeastern hemisphere. In 1986 Dr. John D. Pettigrew, University of Queensland, Australia, postulated with some certainty that this flying mammal, unlike other bats, may be a member of the primate family, hence the only flying primate—man or ape.

On the bat's back I do fly . . .—Ariel

Act V, Scene 1
The Tempest—William Shakespeare

Library of Congress Catalog Card Number 86-82187
ISBN 0-9617225-0-9

The Flying Fox Press
4448 Faraday Place N.W.
Washington, DC 20016

But ask now the beasts, and they shall teach thee;
and the birds of heaven, and they shall tell thee:
Or speak to the earth, and it shall teach thee;
and the fishes of the sea shall declare unto thee.

—Book of Job, XII, 7-8

V

Some of the selections in this book have appeared in the follow-ing: *Animals, Between the Species, Defenders, EnviroSouth*, the *National Humane Review*, the *North Georgia Review*, the *Washingtonian*, the *Washington Post* and in the following anthologies: *Columbia Poetry*, Columbia University Press, *From the Mountain*, Memphis State University Press, and *Animals, Nature and Albert Schweitzer*.

Other books by the author

Forever the Wild Mare, Dodd, Mead. 1963,
Animals, Nature and Albert Schweitzer, Albert Schweitzer Center, Albert Schweitzer Fellowship, Animal Welfare Institute, Humane Society of the United States. 1982. (An anthology with commentary.)

Designed by Ann Cottrell Free

Illustrations by Linda Woodward. Also by unknown artist-designers of European and Asian embroideries and tapestries of the 17th, 18th, 19th centuries; and by Kenneth Bird (Fougasse) and Nathaniel Miller.

For
Elissa Blake Free
and
In Memory of
Emily Blake Cottrell
(1887-1972)
and
Emma Walters Blake
(1861-1950)

CONTENTS

I

'THE HOUSE OF LIFE'

II

'SUNLIGHT STILL IN HIS EYES'

III

'THE QUALITY OF MERCY'

IV

'JOY TO THE WORLD'

V

'THE WAYS OF LOVE'

PREFACE

These poems and fragments of prose tell, I hope, their own story, but it is the same story I have been trying to tell since childhood. These selections reflect moments of deep sorrow and bright joy over the animal, nature and human condition — a distillation of tears, anger and an aching heart. They were written over a very long period of time, their message always the philosophy expressed so well by Dr. Albert Schweitzer as "reverence for life" — a beautiful, but a demanding philosophy.

I add these selections, many of them unpublished, to my articles, other books and testimony before community, State and Federal lawmakers on behalf of passage of laws, embodying that philosophy. History shows that poetry, too, can bear witness. It can bring new vision to the commonplace and it can speak the language of the heart, where most meaningful action begins.

This book is divided, in a general way, into five sections. It opens with glimpses of a loving, simple, natural world and the threats against its integrity. In the second and third parts, it offers instances of irreverence in the outdoors, agriculture, city streets, laboratories. It offers in section four a few moments of joy and humor. Finally, in section five, the book presents man's engrained and frightening ambivalence toward life forms, including his own. But it also expresses the hope that this baffling human characteristic can be met in a positive manner.

My appreciation to those who encouraged and helped me bring these selections together is expressed in the concluding pages of the book. Also, to be found there are the sources for the illustrations and explanatory notes.

These selections are offered with the thought that some readers, on recognizing their own emotions, will feel less alone and that others will look a little differently at those unfortunate beings for whom there is "no room, save in the heart."

A.C.F.

I

THE HOUSE OF LIFE

Thou canst not stir a flower
Without troubling of a star . . .

Francis Thompson (1859-1907)
The Mistress of Vision

I'm truly sorry man's dominion
Has broken Nature's social union.

Robert Burns (1750-1796)
To a Mouse

LITTLE ANT

A little ant carrying a fairy's wing
Across the patio, under the swing
Forward, strongward, forever on—
I follow you through grass and valley
Until you have gone . . . .

OPEN FIRE ON A WINTER'S DAY

what red bird—
or was it a mockingbird—
sang
last summer's song
on
this piece of crackling branch
from the old pine tree,
now being licked clean
of memory
by bright orange tongues
taking
its essence
to
Heaven?

WATER BUFFALO—Kwangtung Province, China

I see you through
A thin shimmering veil of Soochow silk
Woven for remembering.
I see you in the paddy—
Soon, beaded pearls, a rosary of
Rice for tomorrow's hunger—
Serene, mud-caked, so very steady
Heading home,
A little boy on your back
His rice-straw hat, a steepled temple.
What more can one ask of
Any god
Than to return as a
Water buffalo?

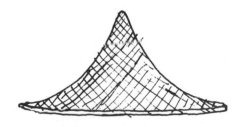

MAY FLIES

May flies, scatter.
Let me pass
And my horse.
We see a brook
Running to the sea.
Tiny cascades over
Moss and ferns,
Rocks of mousey gray.
O, May flies,
Let me pass,
And my horse.

DEAD DOG

Gouged in the belly
Alone by the stream
Feet flying forward
Tongue on the green.
Locusts scream on
And orioles drink
'Til summer fades into snow.
Hares suck water through the ice
And squirrels crack nuts in the tree.
The woodland revolves on steady axis
Unafraid as your entrails
Rot and decay
And your body on the bank
Sinks into bones, then away. . . .

SUMMER RAIN

You smell so warm
And cool, at once—
Summer Rain.

You splash so hard
Down the downspouts
That I almost fear you,
Summer Rain.

Standing water, sudden pools
Childhood toes and squishy mud.
Summer Rain, I love you.

So quick you come—
To last forever.
Then, gone, gone, gone....

O Summer Rain.

EMBRACE

Only the little things can the mind embrace
The kitten, the raindrop, the smiling face.
It cannot wrap its thoughts around
Philosophy, or concepts so profound
As calculus, Kant, or Shopenhauer
For it needs fun and laughter each shining hour.

BEAUTY'S PENALTY

I could destroy more easily
A roach, a centipede, a blue-bottle fly.
But, you—
You there, fluttering
You forbid my mercy.
Why?
Though wing-torn and dying
You are a butterfly.

LOVE, HAVE YOU GONE?

Love, have you gone
As the dew at dawn?
As the peach blossoms
Before the wind—
Silently, surely
Without murmur?

Love, have they taken you
As moth from cocoon?
As the last crystal drop
From the waning spring—
Silently, surely
Without murmur?

Yes, you have gone.
The night air is moist
With tears of distant stars
And the moon is all compassion.
For love, you have gone.

THE NAMELESS

We have no name
For who could have
Named us,
Save the Nameless?
Those Mothers, Fathers
Left far behind:
Protoplasm . . .

But look to our Brothers
And Nameless Sisters, too
Christened by our ignorance:

Robin, cobra, penguin, horse
Panda, squirrel, whale and seal
Leopard, rhino, chimpanzee,
Dog, ferret and rattlesnake…

We cling, Nameless,
To the same
Fast-rusting anchor
In the same amniotic sea . . . .

THE MOCKINGBIRD'S SONG

Let us weep for the wood thrush
For it has flown
And the whip-poor-will has gone
From the night.
Marshes paved over. Spring peepers unborn,
We wait for the mockingbird's song . . .

The world has forgotten —
Or it may never have known,
It has built its own dwellings
And lives in *their* home . . .

I search for a flute, a silver-gold song
That brings music to footsteps
And bells to the dawn . . .

O wood singers, O night minstrels,
Music makers, music makers, music makers — all,
I miss you,
I miss you,
It has been so long . . .

BACKS OF LEAVES

The backs of leaves
White and cool
Mystifying the wind
That blows the tree
Trying to loose them
From their fastening.
The backs of leaves,
White and cool,
Only salute the gale
> For love is theirs, love of the tree.

So, my darling
No wind, strong and tempestuous
Nor forces unseen
Can take me from you.
> For love is mine, love of you.

BACKWOODS
(The Drowning)

The rutted mountain road leads to Heaven.
Swaying field hands and dirt-poor whites
Raise their calloused hands to the glorious heights,
Shout Hallelujah for the saving rain,
Rousing the corn, breaking the drought,
Filling the creek and the pond again,
Awakening the fish, even the speckled trout . . .

Rushing, roaring ,
A sudden flood,
Arms outflung,
Then — finally, mud.

Up the rutted mountain road
The spirits scrambled,
Reaching for God's Heaven,
Sought since birth —
But longing, too, for their home on earth.

WEST VIRGINIA

You speak to me, land.
Swallows on phone wires
Telling me hello and goodbye.
Showing me
Trailer camps and mobile homes,
Red, white and blue R.D. boxes,
Pink flamingoes on your lawns.

Forgotten your red barns,
Faded mauve,
Meandering streams,
Larkspur along the road,
(Saved, by some miracle,
From 2,4,5-T,
Unlike the babies born
In Vietnam those years.)

Speak to them, land—
Oleander, yellow
Sumac and election signs.
Carter, Byrd, Rockefeller.
(What different roads they
Followed to end up on the
Sign on the road passing
A town called
"Omps.")
Grocery stores—all white
Bread, the bran removed and
Only white goo left, hardly
Firm enough for slicing.

Speak to them, land
As you speak to me,
Let them love,
Let them see
Goldenrod in October . . . .

Chipmunks crossing the road
And your will-to-be.

Opening Magic Casements

Goldline darter, Cahaba shiner, birdwing pearly mussel, dusky seaside sparrow, red cockaded woodpecker . . .

Say the words as you will—softly, gently, loudly, clearly. Mumble them, or say them silently to yourself. No matter how you say them, let your semantic taste buds savor them. For they are precious words, opening magic casements onto worlds we rarely see and little understand.

How blessed that little Alabama fish to have such a name as *goldline darter*. A streak of shimmery gold in crystal waters. Then it is gone—fast, able and one of the few of its kind. We have these thoughts, rightly or wrongly, for the very name evokes the image— an image that brings us nearly into the very waters of the Cahaba River, where the fishes swim—and dart.

Blessed, too, that *birdwing pearly mussel* of Tennessee's Duck River to have such a name. For do we not picture—without ever seeing the mollusk itself—a shell so iridescent with shining greens, blues, reds, yellows that it rivals the glittering breast of the hummingbird itself?

How fortunate is the eight-inch zebra-backed chisel-beaked tree climber bird, hidden deep in Georgia's Okefenoke Swamp, to be known as the *red cockaded woodpecker*. Though only half the size of the pileated woodpecker and its virtually extinct relative the ivory-billed woodpecker, this smallish character summons up visions of the Scarlet Pimpernel or a cavalier from the Court of Charles II. In truth, it is one of the more ordinary looking woodpeckers, with only a small amount of red on its black head. But its rarity has elevated it to celebrity status.

And the *dusky seaside sparrow?* What does its name convey? Certainly, for most of us, the sight of the sinking sun over the salt marshes and the sound of a bird. We had only to go to Merritt Island, near Titusville, Florida, for that vision to come true. But no more, there are none left in the wild.

The names of the wondrous creatures of the South keep the language going — vibrant, rich, often beautiful — as have some of its most rhapsodic practitioners: Martin Luther King, Huey Long, Thomas Wolfe — *O lost, and by the wind grieved, ghost come back again.* But the damming of too many streams, paving of too many fields, draining of too many marshes could mean the disappearance of *bird wing pearly mussels, indigo snakes, hawksbill turtles* and *Cahaba shiners.* Finally, the language could be paved over with the concrete of sterile phrases, polluted with the trivia of the market place until eventually it withers away and dies, because nothing was left to fight for or even to describe.

OIKOS

(House of Life)

Elephant,
Whale,
Woman, man
a
tiny mouse.
We all belong somewhere:
A jungle home,
A watery mansion
Castle or cave
a
little house.

Searching, seeking
We are never alone;
All our rooms connect
And when a door is locked
Oikos is the key —
Magic word from the Greeks —
Leading us to ecology.

Rachel and the House of Life

There is not one among us who does not hope that his or her life will have permanent meaning, even if that meaning takes a thousand years to reveal itself.

The meaning of Rachel Carson's life showed up more quickly than the meaning she sought for *so tiny a being as the transparent wisp of protoplasm that is a sea lace, existing for some reason inscrutable to us . . . .*

Her life's meaning was the opening of the door of the house of life for many persons, who otherwise may never have understood their relationship to all other beings also dwelling within the house. She interpreted as few had done so clearly, the Greek word, *oikos*—as "the house of life." In 1869, the German artist-zoologist Ernst Haeckel had seen that meaning and called it *oekologie*—today's *ecology*. They both realized the house's vulnerabilities and that once destroyed, the house's disparate inhabitants would find, in a sense, no room, save in the heart.

Fougasse

Perhaps we listened to Rachel Carson in *Silent Spring* because she was both poet and scientist. We were conditioned into thinking of their points of view as being in conflict. But on discovering her, we realized instinctively what we must have always known, that in their purest form, poet and scientist are one and the same: seeker after truth. And that is what we wanted to be, too.

DEATH OF A RAIN FOREST

Warbler on a bun?
Certainly,
The connection can be dim
For the fast-food cattle
Grazing where once
You wintered
In a tropical rain forest
Warm and safe
After the long flight South
With your young,
Fluttery, foolish,
Bird watchers' delight:
Prothonotary
Swainsons
Vireos, too.
Your home quite gone,
Now, of course,
Many of you.

Don't blame the cattle
For taking your home;
They don't eat hamburgers
Any more than you.
Only offer the ingredients
For those who do.

NO ROOM, SAVE IN THE HEART

Poisoners of meadow and mind
Bull dozers of home and soul
Ready to displace
Destroy us all—
Fish and leopard
Reptile, ape,
Wolf and ant,
Wild horse, warbler,
Worm and whale,
Snowgoose, man
Blind and crippled
Healthy, strong—
No matter where we hide
They are coming hard
They are coming fast
Take my hand, my loved ones,
We cannot last . . . .

In our Lord's house,
There may be many mansions.
But, here, too soon —
No Room,
Save in the Heart.

II

'SUNLIGHT STILL IN HIS EYES'

The hare, the partridge, and the fox must be
preserved first, in order that they be killed
afterwards.

> John Lubbock (Lord Avebury)
> *The Pleasures of Life* (1834-1913)

We must reach the point that killing for sport
will be felt as a disgrace to our civilization.

> Albert Schweitzer (1875-1965)

FAWN SONG

Strong the arm, strong the bow
The crystal stream . . .
And so falls the doe.

Strong the arm, strong the bow
The red-yellow leaves . . .
Mother, I saw you go.

Strong the arm, strong the bow
The November frost . . .
They said you were spared the snow.

Strong the arm, strong the bow
Springtime came . . .
And you didn't need to go.

Strong the arm, strong the bow
The crystal stream . . .
You drank there once long ago.

Now another autumn
Another bow . . . .

FORGIVE THE BOW?

I am too old to be so very young
To feel the tears when the arrow's sprung
To feel the hurt that within me lies
And to forget it's only youth that cries.

So forgive the bow, the archer's dart
And bid "grow up" to my aching heart.

Try I did. It would not do.
Murder is murder—for me or you.

DUSK AT THE DEER WEIGHING STATION
'Sunlight Still in His Eyes'

"The pick-up truck . . .
So small
The load, if you
Can call it that.
That doe, Vern,
Only weighed
Eighty-four pounds
Field dressed—
Hardly worth the buckshot,
Considering those three great
Holes.
Bum shot.
But wait a minute, Vern,
That was only the beginning.
You should've seen the next one!
Had all our eyes shining.
A six-pointer, straight to
The heart.
Some kind of proud,
All of us,
Even that buck!
His eyes seemed brighter
Than that there doe's.
Can you imagine that?
Really, I'll eat my hat—
Sunlight still in his eyes.
Know what I mean?"

FOX HUNT

We will catch a fox.
Put him in a box
And then we will let him go.

I can't capture your fleeting beauty
In the next line.
Nor can the artist create in oil,
The nervous tremble of your body
The fragile bow over strings so true
Cannot reach in treble key
The E string vibrations of your racing heart.
Who then with love and sympathy
Can find the creativity
To save you from the hunters?
To save you from the hounds?

Will they see your proud beauty—
Your russet head silent on the ground?

Hunting the Bagged Fox in Virginia

A fox was born in the western mountains of Virginia. As soon as he was weaned from his mother he started out on his own life of self-preservation, a life which included an occasional raid on the neighboring farmer's unguarded coop. But his freedom was cut short, for the farmer trapped him, put him in a small cage and sent him to some sporting friends down the country.

For two days he travels in a baggage car, eating and drinking a little when the attendant remembers to feed him. Most of the time he crouches in the corner of his new home and wonders in his benumbed fashion what is wrong. When at last he reaches his destination, people come to look at him. He doesn't understand one of the men when he says, "He ought to give us a good run."

One morning, after five long nights in which he gnaws the wood and his claws are worn down from scratching the hard pine boards, the men come again and talk in excited tones: "Man, this is the life for you, getting up at five o'clock in the morning while everybody else is still asleep, but we can't help it—it's in our blood."

Blood of his grandfathers

Suddenly, after being jolted around in the back seat of a car for about half an hour, the fox sees straight ahead of him. They have taken away the boards of his cage. He steps out and does not stop to look around him. His attention is diverted by a sound behind him . . . hounds. Instinctively he quickens his pace and runs with the same vigor his ancestors had when they were hunted on their own battle ground. Between his panting breaths he tries to smell a stream; something from the blood of his grandfathers tells him that this is the only way to hide his tracks from the keen noses of the Virginia foxhounds. He can't find one, but he retraces his steps, applying all his waning ingenuity and courage to these hunters who gave him only ten minutes to run. If he had known one of the perverted rules of this noble bagged-fox sport he would have wished he was a red fox instead of a grey one, because they give red ones thirty minutes to run against ten minutes for a grey one, before setting the hounds loose.

The chase grew animated for those following, because the hounds, as young as they were, were hot on the scent. The master complimented himself on his puppies and their soul-stirring music, for this was one of their initiating hunts.

For two hours the fox ran, hounds close behind him, through pine-needled and plowed ground. His breath almost ceased to come; something within him cut like a twisted knife. With his last remaining energy he smelt water and made for it, but the hounds were then coming over the hill. They saw him and screamed with the ecstasy of instinct. Still he ran with exhausted legs but indomitable spirit. The water was his goal.

Release at last—they had caught him. The leader of the pack clamped his teeth on the jugular vein. He shrieked and tried to bite back. It was over. Now they were cutting off his tail and saying, "The brush goes to you, Jane."

Hacking back to the stable did they compliment his pluck? No. "If he had any sense, he would have turned off at the north gate and found the stream," one hunter said. "It was his own fault that he didn't get away."

LADIES IN FUR COATS

Know your fur by the company it keeps. — advertisement

Let the blood drip
Bright and red
Or maybe royal blue
Since *they* think *theirs* turns
Aristocratic
When *they* are wearing you.

TRAP

Give me a golden trap
To make my life secure:
Husband, babies and a soft fur coat
To hold me in its arms.

KIND HEARTS AND BLIND SPOTS

Mrs. Roosevelt, I do wonder
About that silver fox.
You were so perfect, kind and good,
But somehow about wild creatures
You never quite understood.
But I believe if you had listened with
Your gentle heart,
As you did for blacks, children and
Other victims of custom,
That *neckpiece* you would have jettisoned.
Little foxes and others would have had a
Fresh start—
A life of freedom; better yet, left unborn
If their sad fate
Was to adorn
Another First Lady, housewife, T.V.-movie star.
Those strangely blind
To what happens afar . . . .

HARP SEALS

Sealing—
Squealing,
Reeling,
Feeling . . .
Someone stealing
Life.
So many rhymes
To report the crimes,
Whimpers, whines
On the bloody ice.

SIKA DEER HUNT FOR WHEELCHAIR HUNTERS, CHINCOTEAGUE NATIONAL WILDLIFE REFUGE

The Sika deer lives on Chincoteague,
Not on a Japanese screen
Where it belongs.
A miniature deer three feet tall
From the Orient.
Rust-brown in Winter; in Summer
Sunlight-dappled,
Red, white polka-dotted,
Flaring black nostrils, tiny twitching ears,
Dark eyes, milk-cow soft but
Bright as Reddy Fox's—never daring,
Antlers branching small;
Poised for any predator, come Winter, Spring
Or Fall—
Ready to bound up and down
On legs like pogo sticks.

Oh, use them now — never, never stop!
Someone is waiting for his harvest,
For his winter's crop.
Don't pity the mighty hunter
Waiting there in a chair
The whole day long.
Don't stand there wondering . . . .
Something HAS gone wrong!

One sharp crack from his Winchester rifle
Declares his handicap merely a trifle
As he watches the tiny Sika fall.

A LETTER TO MR. JAMES MICHENER

Dear Mr. Michener, This, I thought you would like to
  know.
At a cocktail-buffet in Washington, the summer of '78
Raves, raves, raves about your book,
Chesapeake.
All the little stores on the Eastern Shore
Are selling it.
An agreeable Mr. and Mrs. I talked to (never caught their
  name)
Told me how wonderful it is to have
You there, living near their second home—the place
They like the best when the Canadas are flying high.
They loved what you wrote about the geese.
And we talked about what you wrote about those geese
Mating for life.
We talked about how well you handled the part about
The wounded goose wife—shot by hunters,
But saved by the gander
So they could fly, fly, fly northward
(Some even over *the* Cape),
Raise another family and again and again
Escape, escape.
The Mr. and Mrs. said it was too bad that man has to kill
  the geese—
Since there are no more wolves around
To do it.
Killing the geese helps the farmers, so they wanted
To give the farmers a hand, save the crops and all that.
(Seems to me I've heard these arguments before—never
That it's so much fun.)

And they also told me that their dog was helping them
Take the wolves' place, too.
They had sent him to retriever school and they missed him
Something fierce.
And hoped he would be home soon.
And the hunting (or is it "shooting"?) season
Couldn't come soon enough.
(Come and gone, by now, no doubt.)
The conversation went on and on— you, geese, dogs,
    wolves.
And then the Mr. of the couple, whose name I never
    caught,
Told me proudly
Of what once he had done:
"I got two geese with one shot once,"
He said that. (He really did.)

Oh, Mr. Michener, did I blow my cool
When I said real soft and low
To this agreeable, partying pair
(Maybe they did not hear.)
"I hope they were Mr. and Mrs.
So neither would be left to mourn—
Or, for that matter, go to parties alone."

Preserving Our Beautiful 'White-Robed Angels'

Just because they are so beautiful should we care so much about the death of greater snow geese no longer flying safe and free over our land and waters?

Some have already fallen. But the sharp pain in the breast awaits the greater number of birds to be shot in coming weeks after they have settled into their traditional wintering grounds along the Maryland, Virginia, North Carolina coast.

Will they fall as gracefully as they fly, stretching across the heavens in great V formations, then again strung out single file? Or will they fall noisily, awkwardly as red streaks stain their white feathers?

It makes no sense to play Shelley weeping for Adonais. It is anthropomorphic to look upon greater snow geese as the closest we will ever get to the angels. It will be wrong to look uncharitably upon Christmas every time we see a greeting card of white-robed angels in full flight.

Should we not deplore as much the mass slaughter of blackbirds and the routine shooting of the widgeon, the gadwall, the handsome Canada goose?

We do.

It is only that beginnings are so hard to accept. And the opening of the hunting season on the greater snow goose — *chen hyperborea atlantica* — after 44 years is surely a beginning.

WINDMILL
(My Mother's Mare)

Chestnut,
Like my Mother's hair when she was young.
Your head held high,
Like hers
Through all those bad times—
And glorious times,
When over all those jumps
You took her to her only glory,
And yours, too, I believe.
(Those silver cups I keep shining,
Though the engraving has grown quite dim.)

You went lame
And all of us went broke,
1929—Depression days . . . .
They sent you to a farm to live,
And the price of grain for winter
Went up,
So they put a bullet through your brain.

Mother never shed a tear;
But her chestnut hair
Went white.

LASCAUX

To the Paleolithic Cave Artists

Horse, bull
Cow and bison,
Graceful antlered deer,
Scratched, engraved,
Painted on the rock of the deep, cold cavern wall—
Your message
Ever clear:
Magic, marrow
Meat and myth
All the same—
Ever, ever so....

DONKEY

Donkey, burro, little ass—
Whatever your name—
You bear the weight
Of the third world
On your back;

Jesus and Mohammed, too.

THE CHILDREN'S BULLFIGHT

Seville, Spain

A meek black bull was the shining star
Of the children's special corrida.
Lots of clowns, even Chaplin, Charles,
Horns, loud music and bouncing balls,
Clowns, buffoons circle the track
Somersaulting, like Cretans, over his back.
Matadors, picadors—all disguised
(Is that little black bull so despised?)
Now what comes next, close your eyes, cover your ears
Olès, huzzahs and wild childish cheers,
Shoulders slick with blood and clotted gore.
From all that sticking, gone before.
Now wait, a moment, here comes Charles
To tease and torment before he falls;
The little black bull can hardly stagger—
Will Charles use a sword or try a dagger?
It won't take much to bring him down.
Three times, Charlie tries—what a clown!
Now again, an earnest, Hemingway powerful thrust!
The kids don't know it—a dreadful bust.
All they want are Cokes, Pepsi, fun and games
Whilst the big mules drag out those small remains.

And there the lion's ruddy eyes
Shall flow with tears of gold . . .

William Blake (1757-1827)
Songs of Innocence

CAGED LION IN THE ZOO

Pacing,
Pacing,
Ever tracing
Misery
On
The savannah
Of your barren cage.

III

'THE QUALITY OF MERCY'

Ubi Saeva indignatio ulterius cor lacerare nequit

—Epitaph for Jonathan Swift,(1667-1745)
St. Patrick's Churchyard, Dublin

'I can't get out—I can't get out,' said the starling—
'God help thee,' said I, 'I'll let thee out, cost what it will . . . .'

Laurence Sterne (1713-1769)
A Sentimental Journey

The question is not Can they reason?
nor can they talk? but can they suffer?

Jeremy Bentham (1748-1832)
Principles of Morals and Legislation

49

NO ROOM, SAVE IN THE HEART
(Overcrowded Animal Shelter)

The big, black Labrador looked slightly
bewildered when he saw the man with the
needle. But whatever was going to happen,
he was going to shake hands first. That's
the way they trained him, before they turned
him in because he was "too friendly." They
told the man at the humane society shelter:
"He loves everybody, licks them, shakes hands.
Damn nuisance —too much for us. Surely
you can get a good home for him.
Purebred, too." The euthanizer finally
shook the dog's paw, swore at the "son
of a bitch who turned you in," and got
on with the job. Then he said, "Next please."

GENTLE RAIN

(Euthanizer's Song)*

The quality of
Mercy
Is *always*
Strained.
It does *not* drop
As
Gentle Rain
From heaven
When the needle is ready
When my hand is steady
And when I can't say
Goodbye.

*Animal shelter

LOST DOG

In warm complacency
I enclose in lines
Hunger and fear on a winter's night,
Twisting cold of icy rain
And a dog afraid
Of a hand to help, corral, caress
And to banish wild distrust.

In my warm complacency,
I write—and I tell you
He would not stop —
Block after city block,
Streets, black and slick
He fled, fearing the one
Who would help,
But he could not turn.

The *beast* was strong within his soul—
Beast made beast by man.
And I cried out to him—
But he fled, fled, down the night.
As my breath cut my breast
And I fled to my warm cocoon.

"SATURDAY"

Little "Saturday" came back in a dream.
Rough coated and red with mange
Whimpering as she was on that winter's day.
You called her "Saturday" for that was the day
You lifted her gently into your greatcoat
And carried her to the country for warmth and play.
After a year on the highway she lay
Crumpled and torn, a little whimper.
But why should she come back in a dream
When it is of you I am thinking,
Lying sick and feverish too many miles away?

INTERSTATE 81

Side roads, daisies,
Honeysuckle
And disconnected numbers—
Different routes—
901, 522, 631 and 749
50, 11, 75
County and State
Feeding 81
Jumble of digits, jumble of dogs,
Brown and tan, black and white
Some fierce, some cowering
With trusting eyes . . .
Dogs, gone, gone, gone far away
Gone to Pittsburgh in crowded vans
Gone to Philly, New York, Baltimore . . .
Gone from your yards
Gone from your pounds,
But never, never
From your hearts—
As you put up your signs calling them home:
Darter, Ajax, Little Sue.
All the dogs
The laboratories want
The bunchers can supply...

STIR-CRAZY
LABORATORY DOG

Beagle, Beagle
Circle, circle
Circle within your cage.
A path to the brook . . .
A path to the hedge...
Over the hill . . .
Down to the meadow . . .
Sniff the morning . . .
Fresh with dew . . .
You have worn down the grid
But never quite through.

LAB ATTENDENT'S CONFESSION

"The Lethal Dose-50
Is not so nifty
When you begin to watch.

The L.D.-50
Is not so thrifty
When you hear their cries.

Force-fed creatures
Are the awful features
Of this terrible test.

Testing chemicals for pills and food
To find if very bad or very good
It's enough to make you sick.

With each convulsion
I feel revulsion
And pity for the rat.

Spare me the hounds
And their moaning sounds
In a room not far away.

The L.D.-50
Drives you to whiskey
Before half the animals die.

This is my tale—
Sharper than a Jesus nail
Pinning them to the cross."

LISTEN WITH YOUR THIRD EAR

Anthropomorphic?
Surely, I am
And
Certainly, indeed,
Are you.
The more the monkey, mouse, chimpanzee
Is like a human being
The more useful it is for you
To cut, inject ,
Burn, slowly starve
And always imprison
To watch and study their reactions
To try to apply to man.
But the cry I hear
You hear, too.
For me, a screaming call for mercy
For you a squeaking wheel,
A tool loudly vocalizing
In need of lubrication...

But listen again with your third ear
You don't need the other two.
Listen with the ear of your awakening soul
And you may hear your own voice asking,
What am I to do?

PET-SHOP MONKEY — Owner's Dilemma

The man at the pet shop
Four long years ago
Never told me
How you would
Grow—powerful,
Angry—longing for
A jungle, a branch
To swing on,
A mate to win.
What must I do?
You do so shake your cage.
The bars might bend,
You seem so strong.
The zoos don't want you,
And the laboratories—No,
No, never, No.
Would you rather stay?
Stay like this,
Behind bars,
So Angry?
Or drift away
(Pill and needle)
To jungles
You saw with
Mother before she fell,
Clutching you
To her breast?

LAB ANIMAL'S PRAYER,
SEEKING SUBSTITUTES

Mr. Henry Ford,
With your Model T
You made the world safe for
Black Beauty
Now, some one, somewhere
Please, do the same
For me.

WHY?

Why am I so fierce?
Because I am so gentle.

Why am I so angry?
Because I so love peace.

Why am I freeing these animals?
Because I want so much to sleep . . . .

BUNNIES

I saw a sign by the road—
A sign I'll never forget:

good For Food
oR
AN AdoraBle pEt

CHURCH PICNIC

So lately a ball of
Chirping
Yellow fluff,
My tiny friend.
You grew;
Your wings fluttered
When I lifted you.

Now the preaching's done
And the afternoon is filled
With drumsticks in cornmeal batter
Fried.

Oh, No.
Not You?

RITES OF AUGUST

We go to the animal fair,
4-H members are certainly there;
Parading their steers
Before auctioneers,
Feeding their hogs,
Petting their dogs,
Combing their lambs—so snowy white.

They've won their ribbons
And got a good price,
So now the time has come . . . .

Say a prayer,
Finger your beads,
Seek guidance from above.

Dear God:
Save the animals. Make them late.
Please, please
Keep them from their final fate.

ABSOLUTION FOR THE SINNING LAMB

The Governor entered the livestock ring at the State Fair
when he saw the young girl owner of the prize-winning market
lamb burst into tears. The lamb would soon be converted into
premium chops and roasts. — News report.

"The lamb is pardoned,"
The Governor proudly
Proclaimed.

"Its crime? Its crime?
Let me think,
Let me see . . .

"Who did it stab?
Who did it slay?
Forgive me, forgive me
I've quite forgot . . .

"Whoever or
Whatever . . .
Just let it be,
For now sweet Angela's tears
Have set him free . . . ."

CHARLIE

Hello, my name is Charlie. I am a pork chop
and I live at Bill Smith's farm—Sign on a
pig's pen at 4-H swine barn at County Fair.

Pork chop blues,
That's what's news.
A sad little pig
Growing so big
That he's nobody's pet
Anymore.
His name's not Wilbur
And no Charlotte's around,
But, wait a few hours:
The killing ground.

HOG HEAVEN

*(A factory farm pig's thoughts
on the way to slaughter)*

If "death hath 10,000 doors",
As the poet wrote,
Let me try but one:
A sudden veil
A sharpened knife
Bleed me out . . .
Into an endless dream
Never waking to live my life again —
Confined, confused and
Without a friend.

Take me on to Paradise…

FACTORY CHICKEN FARM

The long, low houses
On the Eastern Shore
Facing endless,
Faceless infinitude . . .
Until, finally, the
Face of
Frank Perdue
Faces you.

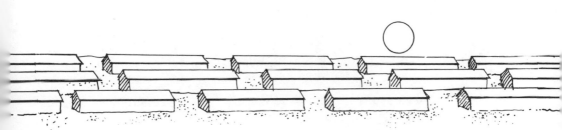

PREACHER IN THE FACTORY FARM BELT

De-beaked
De-tailed
De-horned
A crime
A blasphemy
Idiots' delight
I dared to preach
Now
De-frocked!

MESSAGE

From a genetically-engineered beefelephant

I am well mixed up with this gene or that,
Making me grow big and lean — never fat;
No cholesterol! For this a bow, a mighty cheer,
My master, my mentor, mother-father, *my engineer.*
But on one little item you made a huge snafu
You gave me a heart that keeps saying "I love you."

I can only cry out as you go to "put me down" —
Please, a small heart (like yours) next time 'round . . . .

A VEAL CALF'S THOUGHTS

Veal brains
Wrapped in plastic
On the meat counter,
What do you *think* of
Us?

IV

'JOY TO THE WORLD'

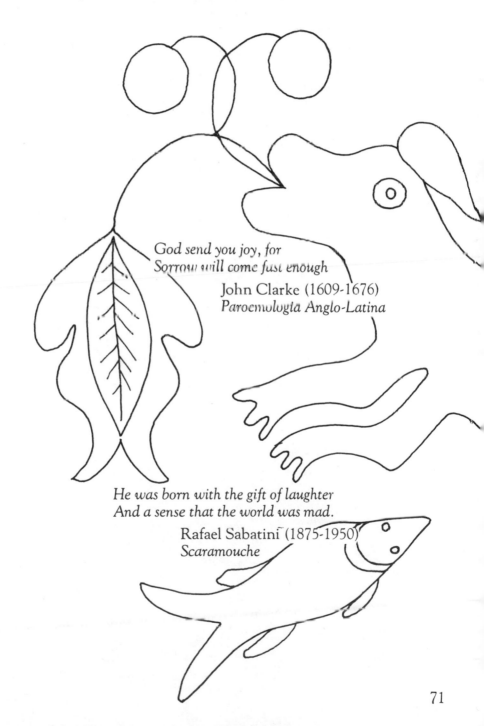

God send you joy, for
Sorrow will come fast enough

John Clarke (1609-1676)
Paroemologia Anglo-Latina

*He was born with the gift of laughter
And a sense that the world was mad.*

Rafael Sabatini (1875-1950)
Scaramouche

Qui me amat, amat et canem meum.

St. Bernard (1090-1153)

CARIBBEAN

Underwater at Lovango Cay Pelican Sanctuary

"Coral brain,"
They call you.
Through your trepanned skull
Silver mini-minnows
Faster
Than fleeting thoughts
Flash
In glittering schools,
Dart
Through the cranium
That is you—
While black and yellow-striped
"Sergeant major" sentinel fish
Mistake them
For frightful mini-minnow schemes
And guard you extra well;
While seafans—
Lavender, pink, orange, blue—
Fan gently,
Like Southern ladies
On broad verandahs
Waiting for the dinner hour,
When suddenly
Young pelicans
Diving—learning at their mothers' knees—
Gulp those mini-minnowed
Fleeting thoughts
Just in time,
Before they grow too dangerous
And change the world!

KITTY LITTER

Our Kitty uses the zinnias' bed.
Seedlings now, but soon blossoms—pink and red.
O Kitty, don't. We love you much,
But how can you treat the zinnias such?

SLEEPING CAT

O black velvet, supple and smooth
Curled so gracefully for a snooze
What do you dream about
You dreadful cat?
Killing birds and all of that?

JANE GOODALL

Rebel in Academe

Jane Goodall caused much despair
Had her professors tearing their hair.
My, my what a dreadful bungle,
Could she think she was still in the jungle?
For them an animal was always an "It",
Her outlandish ways gave them a fit—
By insisting on "She" and sometimes "He"
When writing about the chimpanzee!

DOGGEREL

Oh why, Oh why do I relate to dogs?
I am not one, you know.
But something happens when I see
A little pup of high or low degree.
It may be the sniffing of the nose,
Cocking of the ear
Or perhaps the wiggle-waggle
Of its fuzzy little rear.
Licking, chewing, barking mutts
Cuddly, naughty balls of fluff,
Solid, languid St. Bernards
Or whippets sharp and clear.
Salukis, silken, slinky, baffle me,
But not those poodles of aristocracy.
Schnauzers, gigantic, of ancient stock
Like Brahms, Beethoven, and J.S. Bach.
Bassetts, droll, with ears that flop
The list goes on—will never stop.

So, I'll call the roll—
"Come, take a walk,
Punch and Judy, (how you did bark!)
Missy, Scamper, Angel dear,
Billy, Barely, old Chipper-choo
Zolo, Heathcliff and Bitsy, too."

Some do not answer, for they are gone,
Others, ready and willing come on call.

So many good friends over the years,
Bringing love and joy—but farewell tears.

TENNIS, ANYONE?
(15th Century)

Tennis—a cruel sport?

The ball wrapped in a dog skin
And bounced against a gut.

ANTS

Ants—a question:
Do you sleep at night like me?
And wake with the chipping sparrow in the tree?
Or do you always hurry, helter skel,
Like other souls eluding hell?

ECHO

There's an echo chamber
Inside my heart
Where all your words* reside.
I listen to them
One by one,

      by one,

            by one,

                 by one,

                     by one,

                         by one,

                             by one . . .

It's like having you
At my side.

* *(Reader may substitute: barks, meows, whinnies, moos, roars, chirps, hisses, or any other desired animal sounds.)*

LONELINESS

Loneliness
Has many bedfellows;
But
They have all turned over.

CREDO

I do not believe in the status quo.
Like a stagnant pool, it cannot grow.

DUNG BEETLES AT IMI N'IFRI

Middle Atlas, Morocco

Deep in a canyon
Under a formidable arch
The Honorable
The Humble
The Harmless
Dung Beetle
Labors—
Important only to him/herself
Conscientious, meticulous
Humorless, never tiring
Creating
A work of art
From the manna above
Dropped by black birds
Under the arch.
An ever-growing orb—a perfect ball
Made by turning it over
And over and over again
Dwarfing its maker.
A true masterpiece—
Winter's store
Three billion balls
Superburger size—
Worthy, indeed, of a
Golden-arch prize.

QUESTION?

Dr. Schweitzer,
Mrs. R.,*
Rachel Carson,
I wonder where you are?
Together talking,
Fighting hate?
Doing your best
To set
Your new world
Straight?

*Eleanor Roosevelt

DRAGON FIRE

For those who stalk me with gun and spear.
Here is my message—loud and clear:

I am no good for eating
Or for making into shoes
I am an unwilling candidate
For any of your beastly zoos.
I won't pull your heavy wagons
Or turn silly somersaults;
Hand my body over to men-in-white
For the studying of my faults.
I am so unversatile, I can't even bounce a ball
In fact, I am good for nothing,
Good for nothing at all.
I am just a little ole dragon without a famous name
All I have is my tongue—
My tongue of searing flame,
I am quite ready to sizzle you,
Burn you to a crunch
Or serve you up, if necessary,
For a tasty, crispy lunch....

THE FLYING FOX

*Scientists are postulating that
this bat may be a member of the
primate family.* — News reports.

The Flying Fox, believe me,
Is a certain kind of bat
But if I tell you it's our primate cousin,
You'll tell me to eat my hat.
But this is the time for thinking
Quite revisionary thoughts
About bats, dinosaurs and other creatures
Of weird and wonderful sorts.

Scientists are out there digging, measuring, thinking
(Or whatever scientists do),
So now old canards are sinking
And we can consider things anew —
Wasps, spiders, snakes, mosquitoes
Deserve a second look.
We can stop downgrading roaches
For who knows what fresh approaches
Are being made to our family, tree
With all its branches blossoming
In ways so re-vis-ion-ary . . . .

GOODBYE

Like the great bull frog
In the Kalahari Desert
I survive the dry season
In my strange cocoon
Below the parched river bed
Waiting
For years, if need be,
For a rain shower.
I leave you now . . .
Love must wait.

V

'THE WAYS OF LOVE'

Love, Your Magic Spell Is Everywhere
        —Popular Song, 1930's

All men naturally hate each other.
            Blaise Pascal (1623-1662)
            Pensees—XIV

*The ways of love are two: love and want of
love. That is all.*

            Mencius (372-289 B.C.)

ATTENDANCE AT A MAHATMA GANDHI PRAYER MEETING, NEW DELHI — SUMMER OF TRANSFER OF POWER, 1947

Yes, I saw Gandhi —
Like seeing Shelley plain —
Leaning heavy on the virgins' shoulders
So *his* could support the world.

ON HUMAN NATURE

You Masters,
You Matrons,
You Wardens,
You are all
The Same—
Power mad, cruel,
Not quite sane.
Self-hating tyrants
Venting your spleen,
Lying and bowing
When you are seen.
I hate you.
I hate you.
But what can I do?

Take your jobs
and
Become like you?

BAG LADY

Bag Lady, Bag Lady
Where have you been?
Up to the stars
And back down again.

But Bag Lady, Bag Lady
What did you find?
A spun glass princess
With a tanglewood mind.

Oh Bag Lady, Bag Lady
Why do you roam?
I look in my bag
And find a good home.

And Bag Lady, Bag Lady
Where do you sleep?
On a pink bench in the park
My bags in a heap.

Bag Lady, Bag Lady
Just what do you do?
Serve as a warning—
It could happen to you.

TOKEN GESTURE

Growing Up in Richmond, Va .

"How long, *Miss* Ann, How long?
How long? How long?"
She asked as she mended my clothes.
Nothing more.
Such questions never, never arose.

Sitting in the back of the bus.
How long? How long?
Drinking from the "colored" fountain.
How long? How long?
Using our back door instead of the front.
How long? How long?

As she left, I did say this,
"Please, call me Ann,"
And threw her a kiss . . . .

FAMINE IN HUNAN

Glistening rice bowls
Blue and white
Porcelain perfect
From licking
When chopsticks
Could find no more
Rice, even a trace,
To keep you
From lying there
Longside your bowl,
Empty as your
Glistening eyes.

NO ROOM, SAVE IN THE HEART
(Nursing Home)

Lost
In the kitchen midden
Of mindless memory:
Silken shard
Beetle's wing
Dance-card tally, tissue thin
Who was Gerald? Who was Jim?

"Wake up now,
Raise your head.
Here's a tiny friend
Who's not dead.
Hold her now.
She's alive and real.
A tiny kitten —
A ball of fluff.

Oh, you do remember?"

Yes, why yes
Her name was 'Puff'.

DEATH OF A FRIEND
IN HOME FOR THE BLIND

Shining corridors
Polished high
Glistening gloss;
Bright cretonnes
Blazon
At your window
Unseen by you,
Huddled in your
Sparse memories
That couldn't keep
You warm, much
Past 92—
Memories
Worn thin from
Remembering
And no new ones
In the making.

RIDDLE

Stream across the horizon,
Skirts cupped behind,
Toe touching turf,
And heel in the clouds.
This is the way to Heaven,
And this is the way to Hell.
Tremble with the falling dove
As its wings begin to flutter,
And soar with the eagle
As it lifts the bleating lamb.
Which is the way to Heaven?
Which is the way to Hell?

DYING DOG AT TOWN DUMP

Vieques Island, Puerto Rico — 1987

You wear Lazarus' sores
On your
Pain-racked body,
Quivering in the Caribbean sun.
Call, call, call for Lazarus
(He may remember.)
You helped him once,

He will not come,
For he is us,
Licking our own sores . . . .

SHAKESPEARE AND THE DOGS OF LEAR
Act III, sc.iv—King Lear

Shakespeare, did you feel the caressing breezes
Susurrus in their softness
And the tickling of Titania's wand
Upon your fanciful ear when you dipped
Your quill into blueberry wine
To spell the enchantment of the forest?

Shakespeare, did you burn with madman's rage
When dark Othello wound his fingers
Around Desdemona's milky throat
And when Hamlet, bleeding, soul disordered,
Saw the queen, his mother, poisoned, fall
Calling his name?

Shakespeare, did you darken your shades in grief
When Richard spoke of graves and epitaphs,
And did you tremble with the parting lovers
Upon the rose-decked balcony?

And Shakespeare, bard of high-passioned moments
Of forest and throne, drawing forth syllables
Soaring in bright joy, somber in black mourning,
Did you brush away a tiny salty tear
When your mad Lear, once regal, now ragged, raging,
So frightened his small dogs that—barking—
They knew him not: "Tray", "Blanch", and ah, yes
"Little Sweetheart"?

The Heath Hen and Peter Rabbit

S ic transit both the heath hen and Thornton Burgess. The heath hen, as all poultry-minded persons know, is no Cornish hen, Rhode Island Red or little Blue Hen from Delaware. And Thornton Burgess, though a writer about the eternal verities as seen by Peter Rabbit and his friends, is no kin to Thornton Wilder.

The heath hen is—or better put, *was*—a member of that game bird family, whose name, grouse, conjures up visions of portly and moneyed gentlemen in knickerbockers, mighty shotguns in hand, going onto the heath from some Wuthering Heights. But it was not only the rich who massacred the once plentiful heath hen (which remains, on paper, still a hen, even when not.) It was everybody. Its extinction was democratic anyway. But who would have thought that the heath hen would go the way of the passenger pigeon, the Carolina parakeet—or that wonderfully euphoniously-named bird, who must have been born to expire so as to give us the phrase, "dead as a Dodo"!

But now scan the skies, search the heath and pray for miracles, but no heath hen shall you find. It has gone and the man who saw the last one has now gone, too. That was Thornton Burgess. He was born on January 14, 1874. It was at Martha's Vineyard, Massachusetts, the last stand of the heath hen of the entire world, that Burgess saw the last bird. He wrote of that moment in a manner far different from his accounts of the tribulations of Peter Rabbit, Reddy Fox and Farmer Brown.

He rarely reached such heights of poignancy in *Old Mother West Wind* or in his 70 books and 15,000 stories. But in them, he prepared fertile ground for understanding the significance of that bird, who, in 1930, spread his wings and danced, seeking in vain the mate who wasn't there and never would be.

Burgess saw the last bird

"It was sheer stark tragedy. Watching that lone bird displaying all his charms, calling for a mate after the manner of his race down through thousands of years, and while I knew that nowhere in the world was there a mate or even a companion for him, that I was watching the very end of one of Nature's creative experiments down through the ages, bathed with infinite pathos a scene that should have been fascinating and delightful. A form of wild life had failed utterly in adaptation to changed conditions brought about by the advance of civilization. Man the destroyer had once again overcome Nature the creator."

So now the old gentleman from Laughing Brook, Massachusetts, like the heath hen, has gone from the scene, we content ourselves with the thought that his animal stories, like stuffed brown bears, will remain a part of childhood.

Blessed is the child, or grownup, who can open to a page that fairly sings: *Old Mother West Wind came down from the Purple Hills in the golden light of early morning. Over her shoulder was slung a bag—a great big bag—and in the bag were all of Old Mother West Wind's children, the Merry Little Breezes.*

WE CANNOT CHOOSE

A surge of sweetness like clover,
Before the honey the bee has made,
Sweeps over me, fresh and large
As the summer sky is blue
And grass is grassy-green in Spring
When all begins anew
And no one thinks of sweet
Endings we cannot choose.

BEWARE

If it's to dry eyes you've become addicted,
Beware, your soul will become constricted.
Since you don't know what tomorrow will hold
Why are you so nobly, stubbornly bold
As to clutch the dust of a departed dream
And to forget there is a scheme
For everyone who will finally admit
That shedding a tear is part of it?

SAINTS, PLEASE COME MARCHING IN

Saint Bernard, John of Chrysostom,
Cuthbert, Basil, Saint Jerome,
And, of course, Francis of Assisi.
The animals need you now
You are quite long overdue
You cannot rest on your withering
Laurels.
Come, and help anew; seek another way
To end the more sophisticated crimes
Than those visited upon your animal
Sisters and brothers
In those far-off ancient and medieval times.
Rise from your graves, put on your sandals
Throw on your robes, take up your rods, your staffs
And come forth marching, marching strong
Music from the heavens, trumpets and cymbals —
Never, never such a band...

There's much to learn as you march along
Many hard sights to see —
Hogarth's wretched dogs of 1732
Cats hanging from gibbets
Pigs, dressed like men, burned
By the stake's orange, licking flames
For their rooting crimes —
But we have not come much further...
As you will quickly judge.

Harlow's monkeys denied their mothers
Cages as cruel as in any age
Worse than those putting Blake into a rage.
Sows, hens, agile chimpanzees
And staring, moaning caged baboons.
Nervous rats bred for anxiety,
Mice caught in traps of glue,
Kangaroos turned into running shoes.
Whales bleeding, thrashing from harpoons,
Sables, martens held fast in leghold traps,
Beagles and monkeys, bodies radiated,
Coyotes convulsed by poison 1080,
Cast-off smart apes that once communicated,
Lonely, armless monkeys from Silver Spring.
Dolphins trying to tell us something
As they, gasping, finally drown.
Pause, O Saints, look no further around…

Bernard, John, Cuthbert, Basil, Saint Jerome ;
The man from Assisi, too,
Make a great noise, a terrible din
Awaken the sleeping—above, below.
Make them forget problems with original sin.
Reach for Lord Buddha, Mohammed, Maimonedes, Billy Graham,
All the Popes, your Jesus—and Jerry Falwell, too.
March abreast and the world will follow.
Just keep *marching, marching, marching in*....

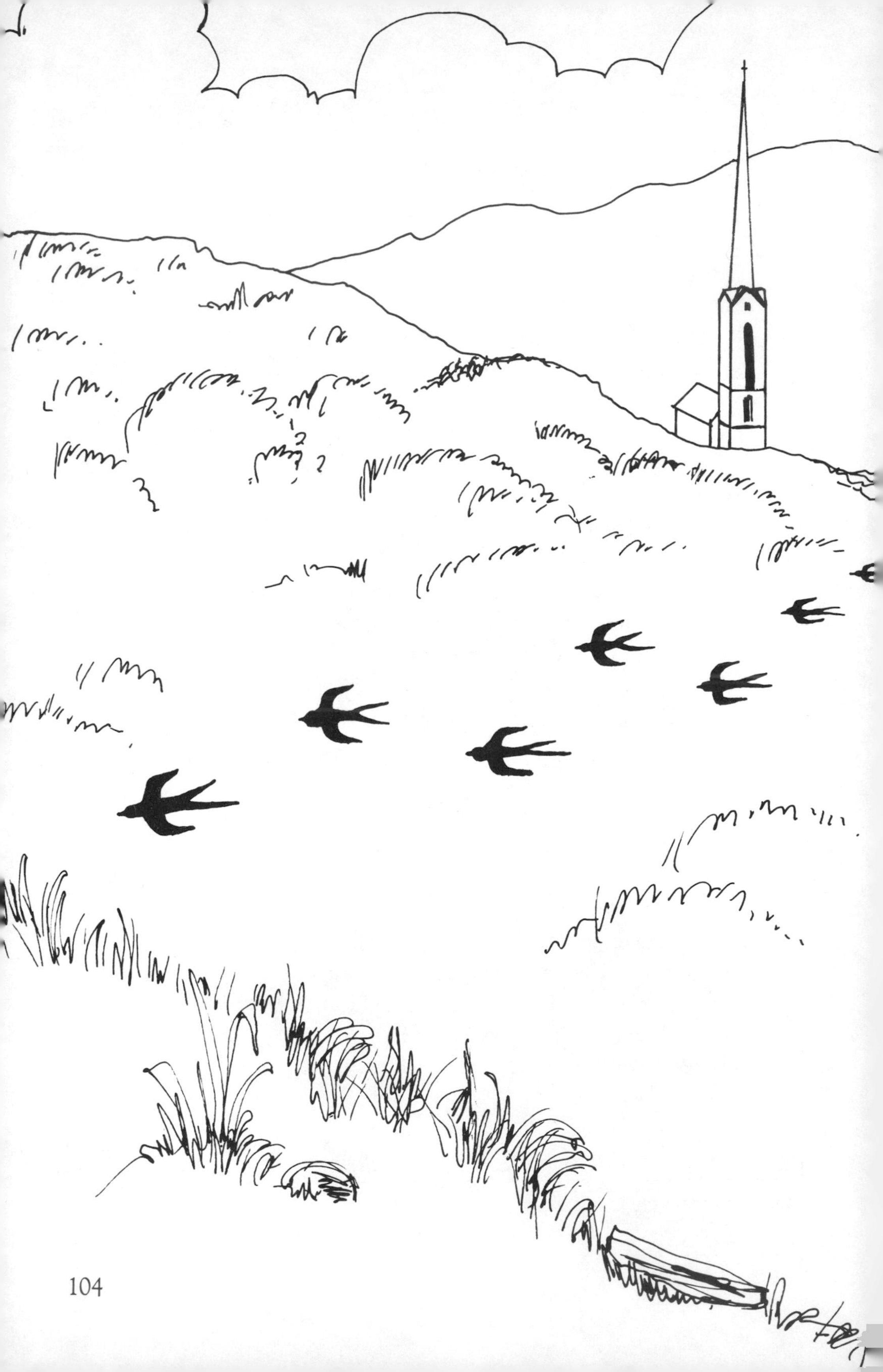

SWALLOWS

We will set out together—Albert Schweitzer

In my Vosges with its steepled churches
The Blue Ridge and
At Capistrano
You gather together—
A bivouac
In the battle of life,
A family reunion
Taking strength from one another
Darting, swerving, curving, skimming, diving
Flying fast –
Faster than a thought—
Due South to
Africa, Brazil, Mexico
Beaks wide open so you can swallow
Lacewings, mosquitoes, little wasps
To add a link to the chain of life,
To help the bluebells grow
Bringing grace, fine elegance
With your muted colors.
Each of you has *your* Lambaréné
And you do what
You have
To do . . . .

The Will to Live . . . .

Not unlike many children, the young Albert Schweitzer questioned in a child's clear and innocent way the mysterious paradox of life divided against itself.

Not unlike many children, he questioned why his own will to live and to be free of pain should ever be in conflict with the same eager will cherished by a deer, a cow, a pig, a dog, a cat, a horse, a mouse, a bird, a fish—perhaps, even an insect.

But unlike many children, Albert Schweitzer, who was born in 1875, did not lay aside these questions with his playthings as he grew up and left his childhood home in an Alsatian village.

That is why Albert Schweitzer was different. That is why, also, that one day the different may become the usual.

Etched forever in his memory, the sights and sounds of suffering inflicted by man on animals—creatures that had given so much nourishment to the body and soul of man. To the young Schweitzer, this was betrayal.

OLD BERBER LADY IN THE HIGH ATLAS

(Morocco)

I am one dirham
To you.
And you to me
A life
I couldn't live
But would like to
Very much—
Climbing those hills
No way to escape
The High Atlas
The rushing stream
The calves grazing
(Tomorrow, alas , the animal souk.)
You bend on your stick
Only a little
As you carry your years
And your pack
Up the cliffside
To your clay brick home.
And I bend a little, too,
Using as my stick
Things not so reliable and true
But a support just the same
As I climb
A different cliffside.

THE CANDLE IN OUR HAND

Yes, light a candle.
Keep it burning bright.
Pass through the dreadful darkness,
Pass through the hideous night.
Hard and cold the searing flame,
No Virgil as our guide;
Pass down corridors, rooms locked firm and fast,
Hear the screams, hear the moans,
Feel the pleading eyes.
Leaving the sinless victims of greed and ignorance
We pass on our way.
Into the dark wood we enter
Where the lion, the leopard and she-wolf reside
With spears, traps and poisoned arrows
And other victims of custom's crimes.
O Dante, O Dante — this is your tangled wood
This is your awful forest
Where you charge those animals with sin and lust.
How wrong, how wrong…
Where is the way for *all?*
Where the sun? Where the stars?

We have your answer.
We hear . . .
We hear . . .
The animals hear it, too.

L'amor che muove il sole l'altre stelle.

The love that moves the sun and other stars
Is the candle
In our hand.

HEART IN THE SNOW

I found a heart bleeding in the snow
The heart said to me, as it faded pink,
You threw me here
To lie like this
To bleed alone.
I said to the heart
I did not know,
But I shall lift you from the snow
And into my jacket
You shall go.

As I stooped to the heart fading pink
It melted softly into the snow.

Nathaniel Miller

EVOLUTION

Just
Who
Passed
Whom
On
The
Way?

ILLUSTRATIONS

Illustrations, unless otherwise noted below, are by Linda Woodward *

End papers, adapted by Linda Woodward from "Scenes from the Book of Genesis: Creation of the World", 17th century Italian embroidery design. This and other designs, listed below, are from *Historic Floral and Animal Designs for Embroiderers and Craftsmen*. Suzanne E. Chapman, Dover Publications, Inc. 1977. The designs, unless otherwise noted can be found in the Department of Textiles collection Museum of Fine Arts, Boston.

Page 1. Flower. French embroidery. 1798.

Page 12. Whale. English embroidery. 17th century.

Page 18. Bird. Italian embroidery. 19th century.

Page 19. Fish. Spanish embroidery. 19th century.

Page 25. Stag. Italian embroidery. 17th century.

Page 46. Lion. Indo-Portuguese embroidery. 17th century.

Page 56. Dog. English embroidery. Early 18th century.

Page 61. Rabbits. Detail, "The Lady with the Unicorn" tapestry, French, 15th century. Museé de Cluny, Paris.

Pages 71-72. Dog. Spanish embroidery, early 19th century.

Page 98. Rabbits. Indian embroidery, late 17th century. Heath Hen added by Linda Woodward.

Page 100. Rabbit. English embroidery. Early 18th century.

Page 106. Deer. Indian embroidery. Late 17th century.

Other illustrations:

Page 21. Bird. Kenneth Bird (Fougasse).

Page 50. Lascaux Photograph, Hall of Bulls, Département des Monuments Historiques. Paris.

Page 108. Primate. Courtesy, Nathaniel Miller.

*(Linda Woodward is a Washington, D.C. illustrator, painter and muralist. She studied painting at the School of Design, Architecture and Art, the University of Cincinnati, the University of California at Los Angeles and at Santa Monica College.)

113

EXPLANATORY NOTES

Information on possibly obscure references is offered below.

Page 5. Under the Chinese new (1963) Romanized phonetic spelling system, Pinyin, "Kwangtung" province in Southeast China is "Guangdong".

Page 16. The once widely-used herbicide 2,4,5-T is also known as Agent Orange.

Page 18. Adapted from article by the author in *EnviroSouth Quarterly*, May, 1978.

Page 20. Oikos, the Greek word for "house," liberally translated as "house of life," is the root for "oekologie" introduced by the German biologist-artist Ernst Haeckel (1834-1919) in his *Riddle of the Universe* (1899) to explain the interdependence of all living organisms.

Page 21. Adapted from articles by the author published in *Defender's* magazine (July 1972) and the *Washington Post*, (April 15, 1965).

Page 23. Many mansions: *In my Father's house there are many mansions. If it were not so, I would not have told you. I go before you to prepare a place for you.* — John XIV.2. Frequently used in funeral services.

Page 31. The author's first nationally published effort, written at age 16 and appearing in *The National Humane Review*.

Page 36. The clubbing of the infant white Harp seals in Newfoundland has been greatly reduced due to public protests and bans on imports of the pelts.

Page 37. The annual Sika deer hunt for disabled hunters at Chincoteague National Wildlife Refuge commenced in 1978. The tiny Oriental deer were imported to the refuge.

Page 41. Adapted from a column by the author published in the *Washington Post*, November 16, 1975.

Page 42. Windmill was the daughter of a thoroughbred stallion, Dutch Prefix, and an Irish mare, whose name has been lost.

Page 43. In 1940 the most important discovery of Paleolithic cave art was made at Lascaux in the Dordogne area of France. The meaning of the well-executed paintings and engravings of deer, horses, bulls, rhinoceros continue to baffle scientists. But it is generally believed that there was a connection between hunting, magic and possibly a form of worship.

Page 49. Latin epitaph for Jonathan Swift: *Where savage indignation can no longer lacerate the heart*.

Page 51. The title, "No Room, Save in the Heart" was first used by the author as the title of an article on the overpopulation of pets, overcrowded shelters and euthanasia in the *Washingtonian* magazine, April, 1971.

Page 52. *"The quality of mercy is not strained, it falleth as gentle rain from heaven..."* Act IV sc. 1, *The Merchant of Venice*. William Shakespeare.

Page 55 U.S. Interstate Highway 81 extends from Tennessee through New York, almost to the Canadian border. It is used by many animal dealers transporting animals from rural areas to their principal kennels and hence to various hospital, university and commercial laboratories. Subsidiary suppliers, called "bunchers," obtain animals from sales, dog wardens and backyards. A non-profit organization, Action 81, was established in Berryville, Va. to prevent and expose the nationwide thefts and to act as a national clearinghouse on pet theft information. Address: Route 3, Box 6000, Berryville, VA 22611.

Page 57. L.D.-50: Lethal dose of a substance, such as a cosmetic, household product, a medicinal, is obtained by administering, frequently by force feeding, a sufficient amount to kill 50 percent of the animals used in the testing.

Page 59. Before retail sales of primates were banned by the Animal Welfare Act, owners often found themselves with once "cute" pet shop monkeys that they could no longer handle.

Page 65. Wilbur is the pig, raised for slaughter, who is rescued by a spider, Charlotte, in *Charlotte's Web* by E.B. White.

Pages 65-69. The references are to "factory farming" — a practice of confining animals indoors for all or most of their lives before they are slaughtered. Beef cattle are confined to feedlots or indoor fattening areas in the latter part of their lives.

Page 66. "Death hath 10,000 doors" from the *Duchess of Malfi* by John Webster (1580-1625).

Page 68. A genetic characteristic of one species, "spliced" into the genes of another species, thus creating new creatures. Current goal: more meat, milk etc.

116

Page 72. St. Bernard's quip: "Love me, love my dog."

Page 73. Lovango Cay is located between St. Thomas, U.S. Virgin Islands and Tortola, British Virgin Islands.

Page 75. In *The Chimpanzees of Gombe* (Belknap Press of Harvard University Press, 1986), Jane Goodall writes of the reluctance of some scientists, as recently as 1960, to accept her gender references to non-human primates.

Page 84. Information on the Flying Fox bat can be obtained on page IV.

Page 93. During early post World War II years, the author spent time in famine-ravaged Hunan province as a correspondent for the United Nations Relief and Rehabilitation Administration.

Page 96. Vieques Island, Puerto Rico. Two-thirds of this beautiful island is controlled by the U.S. Navy, the remainder under a municipal government. As this book went to press in 1987, there was no animal protection-control program for the countless wandering dogs, horses, cattle.

Page 99. Adapted from a column by the author in the *Washington Post*, July 24, 1965.

Page 105. Dr. Albert Schweitzer stressed that opportunities for service were in other places, as well as in Lambaréné, Gabon, where he established a jungle hospital.

Page 106. From *Animals, Nature and Albert Schweitzer*, by the author.

Page 107. Dirham: Moroccan unit of currency. Berbers are the indigenous people of North Africa. Souk: Arabic word for market.

Page 110. References freely adapted from *The Divine Comedy* by Dante Alighieri (1266-1321). Dark wood: a sinful place; Virgil: the ghost of the Roman poet, who guided Dante through hell and purgatory so that he could find paradise. In the dark wood Dante meets the leopard: lust; lion: cupidity; she-wolf: greed.

ACKNOWLEDGEMENTS

I wish to express my deep appreciation to members of my family for their encouragement in word and deed: my daughter, Elissa Blake Free, her husband and my son-in-law, William Ward Nooter and my husband, James Stillman Free.

A very special word of gratitude to Allan Cate, Bella Chaikin. Karen Davis, John Gleiber, Sandra Miller and Rose Forney for their invaluable suggestions and "hands on" assistance.

My thanks, as well, to Loretta Braun, Roger Galvin, Nathaniel Miller, Clay Lancaster, Carol McCormick, Evangeline Pappas-Flynn, Karen Spurlock, and Virginia Warren. My appreciation, also, to Howard Piekarz, Linda Woodward, and to Dan Johnson and other staff members of the Writer's Center.

Many persons, in unique, but distinctive ways, of which they may have been unaware, helped to bring this book into reality. I think of the late Nancy Aldridge, the late Rachel Carson, and the late Major Charles Hume, Elaine Cotlove, Ruth Hapgood, Ruth Harrison, Roberta Pryor. But there are others, especially in the world of animals, Fay Brisk, Christine Stevens, Marjorie Anchel, Cleveland Amory — comrades in the early days of obtaining Federal animal protective legislation — who cannot be forgotten. Together we have seen the growing awareness of the plight of the abused, the old, the exploited — mouse or whale. We welcome the new leaders who have come aboard, heightening that awareness with their various skills. Harmonious continuation of this new and vigorous spirit among these awakened persons is essential and, indeed, can help to change the world.

— A.C.F

ABOUT THE AUTHOR

Ann Cottrell Free was born in Richmond, Virginia. A graduate of Barnard College, she has served as a Washington correspondent for the *New York Herald Tribune*, *Newsweek*, the *Chicago Sun*, North American Newspaper Alliance and as a contributor to the *Washington Post*, the *Washington Star*, other newspapers, magazines and syndicates. She served in China as a special correspondent for the United Nations Relief and Rehabilitation Administration and in Europe for the "Marshall Plan." An Albert Schweitzer Medalist, she is also the recipient of a variety of humanitarian and writing awards for her newspaper and magazine investigative reporting and for her novel, *Forever the Wild Mare*. She initiated the establishment of the U.S. government's Rachel Carson National Wildlife Refuge and she has presented testimony on animal protection issues to Congressional committees. She is author-editor of *Animals, Nature and Albert Schweitzer* and a contributing editor of *Between the Species*. She lives outside of Washington, D.C. in Bethesda, Maryland.

Typeset in Goudy Oldstyle by Dan Johnson
Writer's Center, Bethesda, Maryland.

Printed by St. Mary's Press, Washington, D.C.